These poems were inspired by:

The Shropshire Word-Book, A Glossary of Archaic and Provi
Used in the County
By Georgina F. Jackson

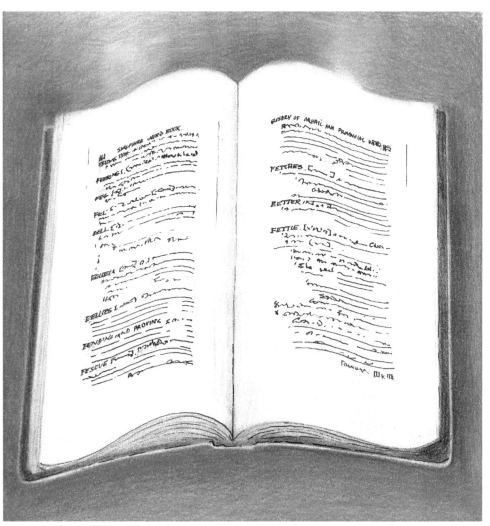

First Published 1879 by Adnitt & Naunton, Shrewsbury
The epigraph for each poem is from the entry in the book.

FAN-PECKLED

Twelve Old Shropshire Words

in Poems and Pictures

Jean Atkin & Katy Alston

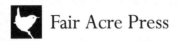

Fair Acre Press

First published by Fair Acre Press in Spring, 2021
www.fairacrepress.co.uk

A CIP catalogue record of this book is available from the British Library

ISBN 978-1-911048-49-7

Cover design by Ronaldo Alvez
Design and Typestting by Nadia Kingsley

ACKNOWLEDGMENTS

Thank you to Nine Arches Press, who first published Clicket in Under The Radar 27, and to Corbel Stone Press, who first published Shalligonaked (under the title Blodeuwedd on the Border) in Reliquiae Volume 8 No 2.

ABOUT THE POET

Jean Atkin has published two full collections:
Not Lost Since Last Time (Oversteps, 2013)
How Time is in Fields (Indigo Dreams Publishing, 2019).

Her widely published and prize-winning poetry has featured on BBC Radio 4's 'Ramblings' with Claire Balding, and been commissioned for 'Something Understood'.

In 2019 she was Troubadour of the Hills for Ledbury Poetry Festival, and BBC National Poetry Day Poet for Shropshire. She works as a poet in education and community. You can find out more, and buy books, at www.jeanatkin.com and follow her on Twitter: @wordsparks

ABOUT THE ARTIST-ILLUSTRATOR

Following a degree in Fine Art at West Surrey College of Art and Design, now UCA, Katy spent some years painting before moving to work mainly in illustration, making artist's books, illustrated maps and natural history illustrations.

As she's often to be found trawling through documents of old Shropshire and field names maps, it felt very natural and logical for her to be making pictures for the 'Fan-peckled' poems and it has provided her with inspiration for her latest

You can see more of Katy's work at katy-alston.co.uk and follow her on Instagram: @katy_alston

BUTS AND FEERINGS

a number of furrows of ploughed land from eight yards in width, determined by the character of the soil.
Buts are on wet lands and feerings are on dry lands. – SHREWSBURY; PULVERBATCH

John ploughs a small farm on two brinks
and neither will make him fat.

Clicks at his pair to steer them up
onto the feerings, and watches soil
blow away behind prints of big hooves.
Here October wind slices like the coulter
as he walks at the horses' tails.
The feerings hold no rain and John knows
even the dog daisies will be scrawny.

Tomorrow he'll plough the wet buts,
on a grey clay marbled with yellow.
The horses will sweat with the weight
and the clay clart up their feather.
John's boots will slide in the furrow but he'll
smell rife earth on his hands. He'll dream
the gold rustle of next summer's wheat.

How's it gone? Milly spooning tea in the pot.
Life's all buts and feerings, says John.

LADY-WITH-THE-TEN-FLOUNCE

the Goldfinch, children's term – CLUN

Lady-with-the-ten-flounces flits
from oak to ash to thorn, she's the one
that hops among the stones, she's quick as daylight

Lady-with-the-ten-flounces spreads
her yellow dress and rustles in the hedge
like silk in the small hours

Lady-with-the-ten-flounces tips up
her red head and all the curls
of rain roll down her back

Lady-with-the-ten-flounces charms
with all her pretty sisters at their song
as close as blood and twice as bonny

CLICKET

the fastening of a gate – CRAVEN ARMS; STOKESAY

Browned and smoothed
by eighty winters, this clicket still
holds gate to post,
the striker bar solid
in the palm of the latch.

Kath's breath hangs on the air.
She thumbs the cold latch open
on a day when silence is weather
as much as low cloud is.

She hears and doesn't hear
the striker slip away,
the gate begin its swing.
She steps where her mother
stepped, and grandmother,
out from working garden
onto farm track, stock path.

And then she turns on the gravel
and shuts it, all without
a conscious thought.

Yet the gate's clicket rings
like a small, high bell,
and holds her in her memory
as if she held their hands.

FAN-PECKLED

Freckled – WEM; WHITCHURCH

Last night there were the speckled lakes
on a sickle moon not watched
nor wished upon through glass.

Then morning fetched a dot-dance in the woods
of deckled oak leaves and the bee-pad
footfalls, pollen-tickled, in the foxglove.

There was a seven spot ladybird
drawn with a pen, who uncased
crinkled wings to fly at the sun.

And in the kitchen was the freckled flesh
of wrinkled Bramleys in the pan,
small-chopped and pickled.

Before bedtime came the counting
of the cockle shells, pale, a little barnacled;
and cuddled on the step, in St. Luke's Little Summer,
Kath's youngest daughter – sweet, fan-peckled.

St Luke's Little Summer: a brief period of calm, dry weather which often begins on his feast day on 18 October.

KEFFEL

KEFFEL

A sorry, worthless horse. From the Welsh: ceffyl.
– WELLINGTON; NEWPORT; WEM; PULVERBATCH

Monty's baccering when it comes about.
Five minutes off to ride the fly-boat, take
the weight off, light his pipe.

Old Royal is plodding on the towpath, just
like every afternoon. Monty blows a smoke ring.
Royal flicks his tail, as thick and white as winter.

His head nods in the collar as he hauls.
The coppice roars with thrushes and the water
shines its steady road ahead.

Wood bobbins rattle lightly round the ropes
that run the length of Royal's skinny flanks.
His ribs begin to heave.

And Monty's on his feet as Royal
stops to cough; and he's jumping for the bank
as Royal's bony haunches hit the towpath.

In the hold is seven tons of Shropshire cheese.
The day's been warm. There's still four hours
to Ellesmere Port, and the horse is down.

Baccering - a horse pulling the boat without a driver on the bank. The practice gave the driver a break, and a chance to smoke a pipeful of 'b

TALKING TO MOMMETS

self-communing in low-toned speech.
'I sid owd Mister Ambler stan'in' in the lane talkin' to his mommets' – PULVERBATCH

Mister Ambler's in the ivy nave, and thinks he is alone.
He's looking at our old bronze bells, long-fallen into mud.
Their mouths are full of leaves, but his is filled
with words. I can't hear right from where I sit.

I hop a little nearer, out to a thinner twig.
I'm brown as a nut, I am, except
for where I singed my breast.

Mister Ambler bows before the bells.
He's telling them their names: Cuthbert, Hilda,
Chad and Bede, Aidan, little Ebbe.
All our calling saints whose tongues have stilled.

I fluff my feathers in the frost, then fly
to find a nook to roost. And I remember
what the starlings say, what

Mister Ambler tells the Farmers Arms –
how Cuthbert, Hilda, Chad and Bede,
Aidan, little Ebbe – still peal some nights
and swing their heads, to chase away the storms.

GEOLITUDES

bursts of passionate temper – CONDOVER

The gravity of rain is like cast iron,
like stair rods dropping through our slates.
The gravity of rain is like a ton of feathers
scattered on the loose and surging Severn.
The gravity of rain spills the Severn over us.

Our gardens go under. Our fields are foxed mirrors.
Our roads flow, like so many little Severns.
In the geoltitudes our cellars fill, and then
our kitchens. Our electrics spit and fuse.
Our cushions float and ruin. Our books ripple.

The gravity of rain is like cast iron.
The gravity of rain is like a motorway.
The gravity of rain is like a coal mine.
In the gravity of rain a half-century of platitudes.
Here we live, under a furious sky, in the geoltitudes.

SHALLIGONAKED

a term applied to a jacket, or such like, for out-door wear; made of light, thin, flimsy material. –
'Whad good ool that fine shalligonaked thing be?' – BISHOP'S CASTLE; SHREWSBURY; PULVERBATCH

Once at first light there was a woman in deep snow,
and a pelt of feathers. She travelled the Portway, far too fast.
And snow whirled out of the west.

Various as altitude and droplet, a drift of prisms
murmured on her downy skin. She ran on light bare feet
and nothing followed her.

On her back, like stubs of wings, lay brown and banded feathers. She was
not flowers but owls. Her neck rotated and
her gaze was hooked and fierce.

Under snow sprung over heather, lay Red Grouse.
He waited winter out, brimful of grubs and warm as fire.
Out of the north, the woman stalked him.

A beat away, he scented death, exploded out of cover. And round his eye
a ring of light, and from his comb
a splash of blood fell onto white.

All day the hungry woman hoots, and still snow falls on miles
of Portway track. Always Red Grouse shouts at her –
Go back! Go back! Go back!

GLID

The [red] kite – 'Bessey, run i' the orchut an' look after them young ducks – I see a glid about,
an' the 'en's under the pen an' canna defend 'em'.

Glid lifts out of the wood
like a loaf rising.
She is more air than feather.

Glid rakes a razor eye
over the weak and the dead,
her beak, a billhook.

Glid rolls a wingtip, slants linewise
over me. She draws the shape
of the hill-edge on the sky.

Glid fans her forked red tail.
She rides the border. How
I wish that I could fly.

The word, like the bird, was almost lost in the 19th and 20th centuries.

NOON-SPELL

the labouring-man's luncheon time – WELLINGTON

Tom lays down the oilcan on wrenched-off horseshoes.
He cranks the starting handle, cracks a grin at the racket
of the two-stroke going, sweet as a nut – suck, squeeze,
bang, blow – the engine smokes on the beat,
and Tom wipes his hands on his kecks.
Then he twists the lever and knocks off the fuel.

Turns to the Shire by the sliding door, who has slept
through the din. Tom's not a man to talk, and anyway
his mouth is full of nails. Strokes down her fetlock, heaves
a hoof like a loom weight onto his lap. He grunts. Mare
flicks her tail. The draw knife winks. The hot shoes hiss.
He rasps the hoof, and clenches the neat equator of the nails.

And in the stink of horn, he's hungry, but it's near an hour before
he slaps her shoulder, nods to the lad. The mare blocks out
the sunlight as she leaves, new iron on cobbles, back to work.
Tom sits down on the bench, unwraps his bait. He chews
and is aware just now, of how the sun, in an odd trick,
is spelling time to turn a man from cartwright to mechanic.

BARLEY-CHILD

a child born in wedlock, but which makes its advent within six months of marriage;
as barley is six months between sowing and harvesting – MUCH WENLOCK; ACTON BURNELL

The bride a little rounded on her wedding day
and not in white, and not in church either.
She endures the shame of the registry office,
all the tight-mouthed in-laws, the let-out seams.

I do, she says, and feels a weak relief, as well as nausea.
Around her, glasses clink and she looks away
fast from the best man's knowing nudge
to her new husband's ribs, and all the grinning.

In the lane, a green spikelet sticks to the sole
of her new court shoe. There are overhead messages
passing in the wires, telegraph post to post.
They find the car, go home to the in-laws' attic.

These things happen, in the countryside, and in the town,
down Dark Lane and down Lover's Lane.
And when the baby comes, it's all made right, it's like
a pact. No-one mentions it again, at least not to her face.

So Steve is born in wedlock, after all, and why dredge up
the past? He's thirty five before his own wife
works it out for him. He can't see why it mattered.
His wife looks at her ma-in-law with something like respect.

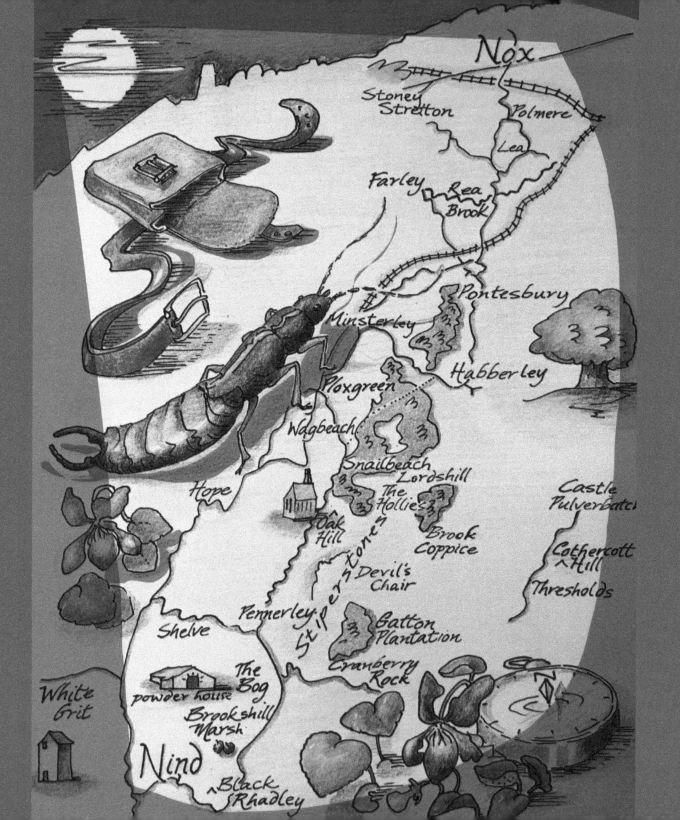

A CORVE OF ODDLINGS

Corve - A large round basket, bulging in the middle and having twisted handles. It holds a bushel or more. – CORVE D.
Oddlings - Things of diverse sorts or sizes. – PULVERBATCH

John fisks from Nox to Nind
or as-you-will, miles end-ways.
He walks in early cuckoo's shoes and slud.
Deep in the candle of his eye, John's
very like his younger brother Tom, though less
a man of iron, more a man of mud.

Moon's up, shim-white and trailing hen-scrats.
She glosses the edge-of-night. John takes the erriwig
from the purse that's buckled round his girth.
Erriwig scuttles off in hobs and girds
but strong. John says to Tom next day,
for Kath, fair aven for another birth.

fisks to wander; miles end-ways a long way; cuckoo's shoes dog violets; slud mud; candle of his eye pupil of his eye; shim-white a clear,
bright white; hen-scrats filaments of cloud; edge-of-night twilight; erriwig earwig; hobs and girds fits and starts; aven promise.